CONSIDER THIS

CONSIDER THIS

Poems by

Gayle Lauradunn

© 2025 Gayle Lauradunn. All rights reserved.
This material may not be reproduced in any form, published,
reprinted, recorded, performed, broadcast,
rewritten or redistributed without
the explicit permission of Gayle Lauradunn.
All such actions are strictly prohibited by law.

Cover design by Shay Culligan
Cover image by minan1398-1654255 on Pexels.com
Author photo by Dee Cohen

ISBN: 978-1-63980-712-3

Kelsay Books
502 South 1040 East, A-119
American Fork, Utah 84003
Kelsaybooks.com

for Quentin and Sandhya
 and the ripples of stone

Acknowledgments

Thank you to the following publications and projects, in which versions of these poems previously appeared:

Fixed and Free Quarterly: "No Jungle for Tyger," "Complicity," "The Lion and the Lamb"
Fungi Magazine: "Bradford Bog, NH"
Lummox: "The World Forgets, Especially at Home"
Medicine for Minds and Hearts Anthology: "Bradford Bog, NH"
NMSPS Anthology: "Unexpected"
PoetryXHunger.com: "Playing on the Styx"
Poets in the Libraries (film project): "Complicity," "Four Seasons"
Survival: a poets speak anthology: "United States History"
World Order: "Inner City," "The Neighborhood"

A special appreciation for my poetry group: Deb Coy, Faith Kaltenbach, John Roche, Janet Ruth, and Scott Wiggerman. And for practical assistance, Denise Weaver Ross and Ruth Banes.

Contents

Consider This	13
Shipwreck	19
At Five Months	20
Hearing the Past	21
Seeking Enigma	22
Bees Have Honey in Their Mouths But Still They Sting	23
Playing on the Styx	24
Slipping Away	25
United States History	26
Beyond	28
The lover who was not mine	29
To Distinguish	30
Ocean Vestiges	31
A Day Is a Year	32
El Capitan, June 2018	34
Breath	35
No More	36
Leave It Behind	37
Leave It Behind—A Detail	38
Cold Light	39
April 2020	40
Sunday Duty	41
Beach Glass	43
Succor for the Dead	44
Flower Moon	46
Listen	47
Contact	48
History of a Man on the Curb Leaning Against a Fire Hydrant	49
But I Tell You	50
Coffee and Beignets	51

Rainbows	52
Near Lake Khovsgol	53
Pulsing	54
I hear music playing	55
Four Seasons	56
Unexpected	57
Nashville Quartet 1967	58
Any Excuse	63
Roses of Sarajevo	64
Famine	65
A Need to Speak	66
No Jungle for Tyger	67
In Between	68
Now This	69
Lives in Cemeteries	71
Seattle 1954/2000	72
Pleasure	73
Complicity	75
Gaze Beyond	76
The World Forgets, Especially at Home	77
Predestination	78
Collections	79
That No-Place	80
The Lion and the Lamb: A Parable	81
Include at Least One Proper Name	82
Where We Go	83
Bradford Bog, NH	84
We see but dimly,	86

Consider This

after Lucretius

I

And then there was murder—mine
or yours—unknown, as so much is. I tried
to follow the line of thought, tangled
in its misery. The crows cawed away. I think
of the many times we passed by a school
and spoke about the lucky children who have
such a lovely playground. Consider.

My heart breaks in morning light over the loss
of you who now float between atoms, atoms
that float within each other, atoms that shape
all forms, all fashions. Thoughts unkind and
menacing. Many betweens exist. Consider:
Acts of joy like sunflowers blooming inside
raindrops. I feel a weight overhead—will
it drop? Only the air can tell us. Atoms
swirl without cease.

Construct our lives into other patterns,
with stars to guide us, to ensure we are
not alone or lost. The edge of the moon
cuts into the night. Consider. The only
common thing is birth. But that is a lie.
The only common thing is atoms. We grab
them at every turn and attempt to switch
them around. They defy us. We are impatient.
A single layer of rain transforms everything.

II

The moon nestles in its halo—a golden
circlet dripping honey. It feeds us. A perfect
circle of life—or is it death that is perfect?
Questions not to be asked as they are one
and the same. Do not hope more than you
love for this earth was not made for us.
Consider this in a lonely wind. The bones
of ancient ones settle in my skeleton. Their
weight is heavy and I would move them
into the rock, not paint them on vapidly
to see them fade in the scouring sun.

Yesterday leaves released an intensity
of orange, yellow, a hint of red, rust
into the clear wide sky. A sky unyielding
in its appearance of truth. Look truth in the eye
—can you see it? I see it behind my eyes.
Atoms bustled again and all changed.
Atoms can do that.

Consider the silence.

III

A scurf of petals drifts along the river bank,
carries its array of colors downstream
into what considerable maelstrom it cannot
conceive. Perhaps Devil's Hole pupfish will
accost them. The distance is too far and atoms
converge in the opposite direction. Or do they?

Perhaps some mythology should be mentioned
here. But myths surround us already in many
forms. Do we need more? Consider the purpose.
All designed to inform our thinking, who to vote
for, which god to bow down before, even though
he cannot be seen. *He,* of course, since men designed
these forms. What were women to do? Stir the atoms.

It is a gambit to move the atoms where someone
else wants them. Do we know where they are?
What do they look like in their present form?
Consider the juggler's game. What falls and what
does not. What bounces and what crashes. Atoms
roll and jump and toss about. They have their fun
with us and we say "Aha, *we* have discovered *them*"
and we roll and jump and toss about in our darkness.

IV

The world is made, yet is being made. Atoms
congregate. Time collapses and explodes
in a moment. All is eddy and purl among
atoms. Consider. The wolf's howl goes
unchallenged. Wait for the wilderness to redeem
us. Remember wolves work together and attain
the upper hand. Go outside to go inside.

Consider who was murdered. Atoms do
rearrange themselves to create someone else.
Which one dies? We find ourselves reduced
and elevated at the same moment. We desire
to be the mountain tall enough to create
its own weather.

We cannot see the black grouse with its
white tail fan in Sami Land. We are punished
for our short-sightedness. Beauty withheld
from us, even the intelligence of earthworms
brought forth by atoms. Consider. Aconcagua.
Canyonlands. Emperor penguins left behind.
Humpbacks gliding the oceans. Impulse
withheld. Art in its shortest sleeves.

V

Our arms entwine. The atoms do not swing
from you to me, from me to you. Each inhabits
its tiny orbit, swirling, swirling. Consider
how dizzy they must be. If we could blend
our atoms, how would we appear? If we
could perceive through the eyes of the great
grey owl, presume what we see there.

Those pupfish, rarest in the world, swim in
Death Valley, all blue and purple. Do not blink
for they are minuscule and dare you to see into
their atoms. Camera Obscura. Its tiny pinhole,
400 BCE. One civilization goes, another comes.
But pupfish stay. Consider what they may have
seen had they been able to flee their lucid stream.

DNA in ancient Greenland—two million years
old—mastodons and horseshoe crabs. Both
beneath thick ice. Melting ice. Dripping.
Only atoms can account for this pairing. But
mother's love is a magic power in the sum
of our memories.

VI

But there was no murder, for atoms
are intrinsically benign. Atoms rise,
then oceans. Consider: Dough is also
a living creature. Fear is a liar. For
the dead do not stay dead. Atoms
rotate, and sunshine flows into aspens,
their leaves quaking. Fear and hope
collide and we come out the other side.
Hummingbirds vibrate their wings. The
music begins.

If a baboon saunters across a rutted road
in front of our vehicle, which one experiences
fear? Both turn their atoms. We hurtle on into
new forms. Damn the dams—in innocence
atoms created these deathtraps. But what
is dying? Everything around us.

Consider: Nature's indifference is safety
for us. We stretch into one another. Worm
sacs. What exists in the silence? Atoms
convert young love to old love. Or perhaps
old love finally evolves in atomic round-abouts,
new again. Tick-Tick-Tick.

Shipwreck

You think entering the sea
        is terrifying, is the end,
                that the arms of a giant octopus

will pull you down beyond what
        you know, once you are wet
                warmth creeps through you. Your

body feels new. An amazing
        strength emerges. Gasping, you
                walk deeper into troubled

water where a new passage opens
        through the coral reefs. Follow this
                and let it remove the dark you thought

hid you. Let the debris of the ship
        float on the waves. Let those who arrive
                in small boats make a home for you.

At Five Months

Does she remember
the increase of her belly?
Her hand soothes over

rippled skin. She leans
her head to an infant's cry.
Can you hear the echo?

Buried far beneath
mother love rocking,
kicking, the babe wrests away

ripped placenta pours
blood. Will she run her fingers
down her legs to mark

the escape? Hers or
the babe's? She strokes a stuffed bear
peers beyond. Nor

will she know. Nor I.
What was meant to be derived.

Hearing the Past

Among pueblo ruins
I smell the past, hear it
trip over grains of sand
with tiny feet. I savor
the fragrance, the dusty
interior whispering to us
but our feet are tiny also
and we can only tread down
the corridors as far as
those who came before
will allow. Sometimes
I think I hear the sprinkling
of words, wise, over
the musty trail. Listen.
Breathe in and forget
the acrid words flung
like lightning strikes.

Seeking Enigma

She travelled half-way to find the beginning.
She wooed the origin of her half-search.

Searches often have half-origins unknown.
The mystery is only half-complete.

The mystery she knew would compel her on.
By digging through sand the half-world appears.

The half-world is a mirage and hazy in scope.
Blindness lurks and dazzles with spirit.

Spirit lurks with blindness in confusion.
Tonight half the moon will brighten the world.

Moon's other half opens dark closures within.
Beginnings begin here in the light of dark.

In darkened light lies the omega.
She travelled half-way to find the alpha.

Bees Have Honey in Their Mouths
But Still They Sting

Inhale. The air smells
    of all the things that have happened to us—crawling
out, digging deep, carrying on. The stars
    whisper of our events. They see how we fight within
ourselves. The confusions, the deepest
    breathing within our own language. How we reach
for touch with fingertips
    that grip all the magic that may be there. In
the evenings I sing with cicadas
    while the world turns in some direction I cannot
follow. Once I held an orchid softly
    in both hands and waited for a butterfly to alight. See
how confused I am. My mind
    does not know butterflies disdain such fragile
flowers, does not know the borders
    of our lives are time-bound. We arrive covered
with blood—going out is another matter—
    we are, after all, cat's-paws of the gods.

Playing on the Styx

Katherine's son left home at 12, roamed
small-town streets, shied away from

anyone who might know him, know
his mother, his strawberry blond hair

hard to miss, that was years ago and I
still think of him, glimpses I caught

of sad eyes, and wonder where he is now,
she would drive around town looking

for him, how did he manage at his age,
how do all the street children manage,

and where is he now in his torn jeans
and Red Sox t-shirt, does he have a winter

coat to pick his way through snow, slip
on ice, find food—with what money—when

she did find him a few times she took
him to dinner, Chinese his favorite, and

he would not speak, would not tell her
what he had learned to escape from.

Slipping Away

I like walking through the pasture,
see the sheep graze, the naturalness
of it all, the oily wool of strong backs,
tall grass whipping my bare legs. Where
I am now is where I find myself day or
night, awake or asleep. I read of Genghis
Khan before bedtime and dream
of far-away places—a palace of marble
and gold, a swallowing gorge, a star-pointed
mountain—I dream you are there too,
in this world of make-believe—strolling
among the sheep. We walk out of the pasture
into ponderosas, wait for the eagle's screech.

United States History

The bones in the fields block the coulters
and moldboards of the steam plows.
　　　　　　—Jim Harrison, *DALVA*

I

Beneath the great hump
and coarse curling hair
bones bend and stretch,
shake the massive low-slung
head, move muscles an arrow
will claim for meat.
Herds four million strong
migrate to feeding grounds
carried over distance by bones
porous and thick.

II

Sitting Bull's Sioux bend
a thousand arrows to claim
the last thousand beasts.
The rest lost to rifles in greedy
alien hands. Bless these beasts
with arrows. Bury these bones
in sacred mounds.

III

Bone pickers bleed the Plains.
Sell for nine, twelve dollars
a ton the warm bones streaked
with muscle. Bone buyers make
combs, knife handles, and refine
sugar. The beast lives in your hair,
your pocket, your Sunday cake.

IV

That was then. This is now.
There will be no cake for there
is nothing sweet in erecting walls.
There will be no grain without GMO.
Your pocket will be lined with lint.
No National Parks with a beauty
that was. The Sioux survive with
tattered lives. We look to them
to the majestic bison
to see ourselves
the shadows we will be.

Beyond

It does not matter what I said yesterday
or what you may think you heard, for today
I stood at the crest and looked out over

the valley. First, I surveyed the dawn and
followed its slow, then faster ascension until
it was noon and the cliff beneath my feet

burned white in the sun's brilliant blaze, but
soon enough twilight came, and the stars appeared,
one glimmer followed by another and another

until I reached out to touch an asteroid hurling
through space, blemishes and all, when the stars
spoke to me from many eons of looking upon

us and I felt voices drifting down on air
currents that soothed my skin, but I cannot
grasp them for their whispers tantalize my ears

and now I understand it does not matter what
we think was said—if we listen, we do more than
hear, for then we can reach beyond ourselves.

The lover who was not mine

although he wanted to be, but the red
flags blowing around him shone too
brilliantly. So young. So fresh. My life
sated. My body resisting. I longed
to stroke his thick black hair, his smooth
face framed by the red scarf around his
neck. He spoke softly. He was gentle.
A teacher of children. Accepting yet desiring.
I let him know it was all right to want, to desire.
Disappointment comes to all of us
eventually—seeps deeply into the vibrant
red of watercolors supporting a museum's
walls. He had to find his desire, to grasp
his needs, but my needs were greater, my
reach further, unbounded by age
or distance. My would-be lover from afar,
escapee from a harsh land, a harsh
government, a would-be lover who wrote
poetry to learn English. Was I harsh with
him? Was I like his government? To escape
he slipped through holes in the chaos
of Tiananmen Square—red streamers
reaching over the throng—slipping
in the blood bubbling there.

To Distinguish

Now, I know
there is no method
to distinguish
need from desire.
I feel the need
for your touch.
I desire your body.
See, there is no
distinction.
I have looked
and realize
there is nothing
to see,
and have understood
to need—to desire—
is to look under.

Ocean Vestiges

It's good to build
sand castles
that we know will wash away,
leaving
only gritty vestiges.

It's like peeling onions
at the beach
a breeze bending the campfire,
fragrance capping the waves.

We've been there
breathing deeply—
those waves,
their white tips trailing
through our days.

A Day Is a Year

1

This day begins with sleep.
Eyes closed. Lids requiring
the room dark. An alarm turns
itself on. Begs for attention.
My eyes open and the covers
roll back as I lure myself
out of the comfort. During
the night a strong winter wind
overturned the trash barrel I had
placed at the curb for weekly pickup.
I shiver in my dense bathrobe.
Later, I look outside the window
again to see that a kind neighbor
has set it upright. Now I can
shower without my robe.

2

All day the sky blinks with winter.
I stay indoors and move
from room to room. In the morning
I nap. I eat cold beans for lunch.
In the afternoon I nap. A book
lies open on the dining table to a page
I have read over and over for weeks.
The words are unfathomable.

3

The need for eggs drives me out
of the house. In the grocery store I walk
the aisles searching for anything
I can find with hope built into it.

4

On the way home
the rain turns to snow
leaving dimpled tracks, dark
against the new white. A
woman pushes a grocery cart
full of her life along Garcia
Street. The cart leaves tracks
upon the tracks.

Coda

I stay home for three months.
Early spring light peeks through
the window blinds. I hear a
scratching at the front door but
it stops when I shrink into
the darkest corner of the room.
Silence organizes everything.

El Capitan, June 2018

for Jason Wells and Tim Klien

It is a wall.
Or, it is a wall on a wall.
Not the paper sort of wall.
Not the screen saver sort of wall.
Not the Ansel Adams sort of wall.
You know where it is by the color of the wall.
You know where it is because you have seen this wall.
100 million years old this wall.
It is rock this wall.
It is sheer this wall.
They died on this wall.
A thing of elegance. Of grace.

Breath

                very large array

maple trees

mottled   green and yellow

bark   a noise

   loud enough to startle browning leaves

burrs

       long stems   dancing

late autumn air

                sun blurring

                    dry turquoise sky

No More

The blood rained out, gone all hope.
The small internal movements, empty of hope.

All parts removed as the red blood departs.
What disintegrates in our hands—hope.

Two sides of happy bond over the bridge.
Life and death. Life. Hope.

The parts disappear in a long, taut year.
A gravel road leads to the end of hope.

Dried blood crumbles.
No rainbow circles the sky with hope.

Leave It Behind

I woke to the smell of evil.
What is that smell?

Evil jars the senses, pinches smells
that cause us to turn away. I've even

seen evil. Prison cages swollen
with children. Faultless people shot

down. A wall that alienates.
That smell.

I dreamed to be delivered from evil.
My dream may have been answered.

I'm waiting.

Does *good* have a smell?
Will I recognize it?

Leave It Behind—A Detail

after C.D. Wright

I stepped into solitary confinement
in Alcatraz. Lights cut. The depth

of that darkness formed its own prison
cage. A brief thirty seconds and we

tourists rushed into the light. Our
relief immeasurable. Our bodies

changed forever. For the loss
of time. For the loss of ourselves

that could not be regained. Only
thirty seconds. What would thirty

years do? Twenty? Ten? Five?
I would look in a mirror

and see a reflection holding
everywhere

bars, dirty walls, a hard bed.
My forever.

Cold Light

> *. . . we have aged a hundred years . . .*
> —Anna Akhmatova

More than two years have passed
but on the first day, and every day
since, we have aged a hundred years,

    have unwillingly blended into millennia
    and there, in those far distant years
    we see not a paradise—not perfection—

        but a burning inferno shaped by thousands
        of bullets, their shells forming the pathways
        we tread. No autumn maples shade our heads,

            bluebells gone and with them the buzz
            of honey bees. Peacocks no longer strut nor
            painted redstarts sing. We shiver in cold

                light, sway our ghostly circle dance—
                I take your hand. You take her hand. She
                takes his hand. And on. And on. Pressing in.

April 2020

The sun lives only one day. Live in a good
way so the sun will not have wasted its time.
—Navajo saying

Here we are—our lives like flecks of feathers
drifting down on us—and we can but hold

on to the earth's spin that keeps us in her
embrace. Someday we may be Lucy, ancient

skeleton, and found after thousands
of years. Departure and homecoming all

at once. A deviation carries us into a new
world that we fear, but without deviations,

how could we define ourselves? The clock
of the universe ticks. We go along on the ride.

Sunday Duty

I've already written my Sunday poem,
written it all in proper Sunday black

for lack of better colors to wear. I can
no longer bear the light that pours

blight through those stained windows
stained with blood that does not flow

even though we are told so, that it
did so. Those windows tell tales in static

glass, stubborn glass, glass suborned
to fairy tales. But if we call them by

cursive names we are condemned.
The crown of thorns is Goldilocks'

curls. The wicked stepmother's poison
potion trembles on our lips as we lie

on the altar. Merlin's mystic powers
fire the fuse that burns us. One rose

bush speaks to break the back of
another, one saint to another. They

hover over all we would endeavor.
I would prefer to pick a sparrow's

feather from the echoing floor and see
Mrs. Chambers' new brown hat fly

through the door for no one told her
brown is out, it has no clout in bloodless

pursed lips, in here, below, where,
even now, black is the color to wear.

Beach Glass

This bit is the bottom
of the bottle, she says,
a slight curve on
this edge fits nicely
around my thumb.
I like the texture, he says,
ground by sand and wind.
Nothing too smooth.

There are no sharp edges,
she says, nothing to cut.
The green color is soothing,
he says, the intensity changes
with the light like first love.
I like the unevenness
of shape, she says, three
sides like a new love
seeking its circle.

Have you ever walked
this beach? he asks.
Yes, once—and you?
As a boy, around 1910.
Yes, she says, I remember.
Before the Great War when
we all thought love
was the only innocence.

Succor for the Dead

after Li-Young Lee

I

Tonight my small son, on hands and knees, crawls
      across a Disney-painted floor
      knocks over toys he cannot see.
Where could he be going in that house long gone?
Does he seek his twin?
His love for me sticks like plaster
      to my swollen breasts.

At this hour, what is old is new
      what is stolen is gone.

Someone tell him the stairs are steep.

II

He cannot find his twin and butts his restless
      head against the crib.
He wakes ten times during the night
      for want of the breast.
His love for me is like his nursing:
      tiny fists knead my breast,
      tiny fingers clutch mine.
But milk runs dry, the sucking is hollow.

At this hour what is succor is suspect
      what is wished for becomes vapor.

Someone tell him the ascent is steep.

III

Achilles, challenger of death, fights
    in his armor of tin plates,
        his sword swings an arc through crusted bread.

His love for another's wife feels like sand,
    like shooting stars, like ice.

At this hour what lives is vulnerable
    what is dead is alive.

Someone tell him his time nears.
    Someone tell him the descent is steep.

Flower Moon

Flowers in abundance
covered the land
displaying
all the rainbow colors
the Osage people praised
in their dances.
What could steal the laughter?

The moon rose bright,
heavy in its roundness,
its light,
but its brightness
was not enough to ignite
the dark pouring down.

The People imitated their oppressors
—cars, mansions, Paris fashions—
those ignorant that wealth
above ground also hid below
in the abundance they coveted,
they killed for.

And the land blossomed
over naked graves
amid tracks of silence.

Listen

Is it too much to bear—yes or no?
        Make up your mind.
I heard thunder roar like an injured lion.
     Did you hear it? Did you hear
           the fear? Did you feel it rumble deep
              in your body?
Did you try to save the lion?
       Here is what I think about fear—
           its purpose, yes, it has a purpose,
is to control us—yes or no?

We encounter its image everywhere
on any screen. Any screen. There are so
      many today
we can't get away. We can't avoid that
   insistent voice. Can't remove it from
        rumbling in our ears.

Listen, can you bear it? How does it get
    inside of you? Will you hand it to me? Or,
will you cling to it, a babe sucking its thumb?

Contact

Rome burned, and Pompeii, and
Arenal sends fiery flows down its slopes

night and day. Yet people live, thrive there.
How do they stay within reach of such

danger? Do they not fear the heat, the chance
of a hot burial? Perhaps they desire

to escape suddenly, without volition. They
make no contract with death, it looms

in all colors, all temperatures. Their resolve
makes its own choice. Fire is the cleanest.

History of a Man on the Curb Leaning Against a Fire Hydrant

He is lean, almost thin, with tanned skin he has carried since birth, dark wavy hair and beard, almost neatly trimmed, a stained white t-shirt, torn jeans, nearly fashionable, black eyes deep-set as though looking at his inner self, as though wondering how he has come to be leaning against a fire hydrant with traffic rushing by, as if he has no place to go, as if he does not know where he belongs or where he can go if he knew of such a place, for he has wandered his whole life, at least he thinks it is his whole life, but he does not know how much of a life he has lived, and tries to count the days backwards to discover who he is and if he belongs anywhere, he thinks he must have a mother somewhere but does not know her, does not know if she exists outside of his desire, does not know if she tried to lose him, for he has heard of this strange phenomenon that causes unwanted children to grow up quelled for want of love, of nourishment of any kind, of any dimension. He runs his finger over the tattoos on his arm and wonders how they came to be.

But I Tell You

No one had to tell me the earth
is round. I can see it spinning

when I look down from thunder
clouds onto a world hurling

into despair. And what was said
to me about this phenomenon

was nothing compared to what
I have lost. Nothing compared

to the stain. To the strain.
Nothing at all to the infant who

floated away. Years pass and he
does not return. He spins but

I do not see him when I look
down from my thunder

clouds, thunder beating in my
chest. He spins, spins as he

spirals into the nova
spirals into that place

where we cannot follow
cannot shine as he does.

Coffee and Beignets

One man rises from his chair amid

    the debris of old New Orleans, extends

his hand through air thick with understanding.

The other rises, hands behind his back. His

lack more clear. He takes a step removed.

    Is it back? Forward? Sideways?

Does it make a difference? The chairs

    remain the same. They have no argument

in this affair. These two have claimed

    the air, each in his own way.

Each to his own coffee and beignet.

Rainbows

As I watched, all the rainbows
I've ever held escaped and spread

around the world in one motion,
ringing around all those I've loved,

all those who, I hope have loved
me. I thought I saw their arc and

reached for purples, pinks, greens.
But they slipped from my grasp

with a whisper of *silly you.* Yes,
I am often unspoken, often reaching,

often seeking change. I held onto those
rainbows far too long. Now look where
I stand, here, in twisted shadows.

Near Lake Khovsgol

I was satisfied at home

until Genghis Khan's daughters
bled their history into my
imagination, how their strength

survived that of drunken brothers
to save their father's empire.
Now I follow migrating reindeer

high in the Sayan Mountains,
forage in deep snow,
stroke their silky hair,

sleep in tents of their hide.
The herders graze with them,
track prints of delicate hooves

from one range to another,
a constant movement of families,
two pots, thin sleeping mats,

meager bodies, worn faces.
Women give birth on the move
to babies of cousins, of brothers.

Pulsing

We arrive covered in the purity
of new blood and feel the nakedness
when it washes away.

My head stays still, waits
for the next pulse. There is no
blood here. Purity does not speak.

Like dust clinging to a rock
blood leaves traces of iron.

Between what the eye perceives
and what light reveals. Blood-shot.

A moment of laughter shared with
a stranger ties us to blood.

Mars, the blood star, marks the sky
and spawns rogue planets. We wait
to learn how to climb out of the sky.

Listen to the Martian winds—they
cast a blood-red light that sings.

I hear music playing

among the trees after months of cold
silence, the joy of new feathers raised
in the light breeze, fluttering. You

down by the river where I take
your hand, newly warmed by early sun.
We walk beside bullrushes, frogs
croaking. I wonder what you are
doing here, but I stay with you, water
rising, lapping our bare toes. Your

hand strong in mine. Our silence
imbedded in music, rustles of wind.
Yesterday you walked out the door,

left me hanging high in the midst of our
disagreement. I did not go in search
of you and was surprised I imagined you

watching the ripples, dragonflies
hovering. Among the cottonwoods I hear
your name rustled through restless leaves.

Four Seasons

For a long time I could not remember
that you had once existed, how you walked,
leaned your ear to listen, held your hand to your

face. Is this kind of memory important, or
shall I let it pass? You once held my hand in both
of yours and spoke quietly to me of how

sparrows sing, how crickets chirp, the way water
sounds after a spring rain. I licked your words
from the air and swallowed them to make me

whole, to let songs breathe from within me,
I, who cannot sing. In my ear, you whispered
your love of all things that creep and crawl,

all things that bloom even in deepest snow
and how mountain elk burrow for these tastes
in winter depths, snow coating their fur

in heavy drifts as they struggle forward. For
a long time we stood where you once kissed
my fingertips under a sunlit sky, leaves
of red, yellow, ochre rustling.

Unexpected

Asphalt parking lot—
a shroud surrounded
by three police cars

and yellow barrier tape.
It had happened in the moment
of crossing from one side

to the other. Pedestrian stripes
offer support. How do we
know when the exact moment

comes? When the leaves stop
murmuring and wind's whisper
calms? Those moments have come

and gone many times with no
hesitation. Yellow daffodils nod
under the barrier. The ebony

asphalt holds a certain
forgiveness—the last bed
not too hard. Not too soft.

Nashville Quartet 1967

I. Then Is Now

Jim Thompson stands on the street corner,
shuffles his feet, pulls his ragged hat
low over his eyes to shut out the sight
of cop rifles rumbling the swarthy night air.

He knows guns make people feel safe
and begins to run toward the art museum.
Steiglitz photographs waver on the walls
between anonymous black artists. There's

no segregation in Nashville. Brooks says
We real cool, while lazy Susans cut through
trigger fingers. Sara Joe thinks it's okay.
Camping with bears in Smoky Mountains,

protesters blow boycott signs, their lips
sealed. Spring flowers melt the air. Empty
glaciers startle our expectations. A muscular
man runs away, his guns melt into pools

of chocolate. Hungrily, she did not eat
the fat rat. Her fingers stroked its long tail.
The barn owl blinked. Beans, cornbread,
collards boiled to mush. Guns meet

sunflowers in a sunset field. My hand
to yours, yours to his, his to hers, hers
to mine. Rifles rumble. Boots stomp.
Glory blooms on the land.

II. Inner City

1

Two blocks away
the foundry smokestack
blossoms twenty-four hours
each day and night—
spewing pollen permeates
windows, Judas trees, zinnias
and people.

Through smoked panes
I watch the hillock of square
crushed cars grow
and take on uniform color
from the unbiased pollen.

Streets bruised from neglect,
interrupted by
tracks. Long distance trains
halt to load cast iron pipes.

The shift change at the garment
factory scatters children
back to strips of pollen bitten yards
and heightens the drone
on the freeway barricade.

2

There's more to consume
than I've yet
tasted but my dust
is dead and clogs
the throat.
I walk into dreams where
shattered metal
blows whistles at
cringing dogs.

ILGWU tags patch
my kitchen floor and

the children
swallow the yard in their
fight for childhood.
I scrub, but the barricade
refuses to crack. I
melt into the pollen.

III. The Neighborhood*

As I lock my front door
(where before I did not think
of it) and walk down the side-
walk—stares penetrate
not my back
but my face
my eyes
directly demanding to know
what I am doing here
and I cannot answer.

Alone in my evening living-
room (thinking it no different
from previous ones)
I am reminded
of my presence here
by the solitary contralto
or bass
occasionally wandering
by outside
free in its
unwhitened soul to be
beautiful and
self-sufficient
not asking me why
I am here—
        indifferent
that I am.

* *Fisk/McHarry*

IV. Manger

The babe in the crib
might be black or white,

brown or yellow, or even
the reddish color

that gave rise to the tag
redskin. Rattus rattus is,

however, color blind.
A nibble here,

a nibble there, tastes
the same. Its long naked

tail trails behind as it
climbs, burrows, gnaws.

Open the bedroom door
and it leaps out of the crib,

runs across your feet.
Its tail a flick of caress.

Any Excuse

And the hare said to the turtle, I will win,
you know, by the hair of my chinny-chin-chin.
Oh, no, said the hare, I will win by the strength
of my shell. He thumps his shell to assert
his challenge. The thump is heard around
the world. Country after country repeats
the sound. All join in the game of the turtle
and the hare. Not only do they play on one
side or the other, they play against each
other. But no one knows, really, what
the game is, or the purpose of it, or who
exactly they should oppose. There is
a difference of opinion about the alphabet
soup of issues: you name it, it's included.
Some believe those who do not look like
them, act like them, are going to kill them,
so they kill first. No one asks the reason
for this delightful ongoing experience, they
just play along for the sake of hating their
neighbor, or loving their neighbor. Any
excuse will do. Some look at the little
men at the helm. And wonder: which
is the turtle, which the hare.

Roses of Sarajevo

      Three days there and all talk
is of the war. Bombs and shells
are alive in their eyes nearly 30 years
later, their ears, their daily
struggle. A city splintered with reminders—
damaged buildings walk streets
spiked with red splashes
preserved in steel frames. Frames pressed
into the tarmac. You can walk
over these roses but few do, for you
are walking on a dead person. No body,
no clothing, only blood fading
into the pavement.

      In a derelict high-rise on the edge
of the city we squeeze into a tiny apartment
housing three adults, three children.
The daughter-in-law is fluent in English
and eager to tell of their lives. Little money,
yet the children grow. Her husband sleeps
in the next room. Twelve hours six days
a week driving a delivery truck. Her eyes
glisten. She speaks rapidly. Across
the table I take her hand to feel the love
rushing through these small rooms.
Children lively, eager. Do they see the roses?
Does the baby toddle over them in her
innocence? We leave and stumble down six
flights of broken stairs in the dark.
Electricity is precious.

Famine

She is present in herself and lets the silence reign
around her. *Look behind your eyelids to see who
you are.* She is here, a woman rebounding
in the silence. She questions how to be alone
in this world where a famine of the soul
prevails in the land.

It is a morning filled with strangeness and she
peers between the curtains hoping the sun
still rises. She stifles the temptation to find
someone to tell of her memory. Dust to dust
settles around the room.

But what is it she remembers? She searches
the drawers, shakes out the bed pillows, explores
closets. All are empty of what she seeks. That
memory lost. That silence ringing.

The tension leads her to search the house. She
feels the tension increase from room to room.
Will she find it, that lost memory?

She has forgotten memory works without
logic or order. Her search is futile.

Famine continues.

A Need to Speak

If I am not writing the truth
I am not writing.

Red leaf of autumn
bare branch of winter
fresh wisp of spring
hot green of summer—
this is truth I hand
to you with morning tea.

If I am not writing the truth
I am not writing.
And still I do not write.
Voices speak.
I smother their whispers
with black ink on white paper.

Truth, the orgasm of lovemaking
the orgasm of childbirth,
of death, that final thrill
of body giving indivisible.

We do not want to know
rain strips skin from bone
food mutates children.

The morning tea melts this cup.

If I am not writing the truth
I am not writing.

No Jungle for Tyger

My Tyger prowls the streets
lost without a forest. Carbons
blast the air with particles of heat.

My Tyger does not burn bright
with or without carbons scorching
tree tops. The Lamb is out of sight.

My Tyger's way is not clear. We can create
our own kind of Lamb, grow forests again,
build a new path to reclaim, to rotate.

In Between

*On your tombstone they put your birth day and your
last day. And there's a dash between. What did you do
in that dash?*
—Jerry Lawson, "Just a Mortal Man"

I wonder how long is my dash,
and whether I ran it or walked it,
where I stumbled along the way,
when I picked myself up
to try again. That is what it is all
about—pick up and go again. Now

I think about that dash and how
many rivers it consumed, how far
it carried me up the rock face. How
many times it dashed me to other
countries, chasing the world.
And I wonder—did I start the fires

that scorched giant sequoias and
vast grasslands, made prairie dogs
hide their heads. I was alive in that
dash, so I must be responsible. I will
hide my head so I do not know. For if
I am ignorant, I am not guilty. And
my dash can rub itself out.

Now This

My love is dead.
  How do I know?
    He has left my body
      My toes trail
        through sand
through gravel   through fire

These things would not happen
            if he breathed

What star gave birth to us?

     We tried once to climb a ladder
that would take us to the answer
    Broken rungs cluttered the path
           He stumbled over them

When have I stumbled?

It is all disappearing

Someone has taken it
        Not him

He is already gone
     Our star splintered

    Swimming does not help
for I fear the tide

   My love is dead

The bones of his fingers tell me

I will walk
through a sea of wildflowers

I will count the colors of yellow

Lives in Cemeteries

I stroll through age-old cemeteries
in god country where Winthrop, Mather,
Louisa, Nathaniel, Ralph Waldo

and all their cronies, and all those
whom history does not record, all those
whom we think did not leave their mark,

who no longer walk among us, molder
among us. At least we cannot see their
spirits that flutter around our ears,

marking us, while we remain deaf to all
their warnings. What good are cemeteries
with broken headstones, lichen-covered,

the names and dates diminished,
unreadable. What good melting into dark
soil to startle hungry worms, assuming

we are here forever for others to come
and wonder at our lives. I think god laughs
at our gullibility, that we do not know

he pees on our graves.

Seattle 1954/2000

A bridge floats over
the lake. Villages
march around
the center—
not a city—a town
of tall blonds:
Yggdrasil roots
the streets. Thor
thunders across
dreary skies
hiding Freya's
sweet smile. The
memory of dark,
of rain, of a constant
sprinkle leaving
diamonds
in everyone's hair. No
umbrellas. No
barrier
from what
the gods bestow.
A Boeing town
where few had ever
flown. No trash.
Shining. Shape-shifters
drift along quiet streets.
Immerse into the landscape.
A Microsoft. A Starbucks.
A Amazon. A town shaped
and shifted into myriad cities.

Pleasure

Isn't everything simple—

        sleep, rest, slumber—

the going into the dark

        my mind at a distance?

Isn't it a simple thing

        to let go   to hold on

whichever it may be?

I hold tight to Orion's

        belt, a simple pleasure.

Mintaka's heat sears

        my fingers. Does such

action change the sky?

Do the Pleiades ponder

    my clinging, my need?

Can I rest now?

    Is it dark enough?

Complicity

In the back of the classroom

I listen to your stories

of war, of soldiers raping dead

women, girls. Of U.S. soldiers

doing this. This. I place

my hands over my ears.

I drown out the drone

of your voice. Still, I see

the nakedness of them

within us. Us. In your stoicism

I smell blood. As red

as loveless roses.

Gaze Beyond

How can you say the sky is not

      blue when even I can see the depth

            like that of your eyes? The way

hyacinths sway in a spring breeze.

      The way you gaze beyond me

            into a cloudless sky. I see you

wherever you look, out there

      where you belong, in the cradle

                  of depth.

The World Forgets, Especially at Home

This black steel of straight lines and curves
abstract beyond recognition.
Set on a granite platform on the corner
of an obscure street amidst the bustle of Lima,
it collects merely a glance from passersby who
quickly look away as though ashamed
they had looked to begin with or
ashamed they do not know what
it represents. Neither did I but
was drawn to the shape of the steel plates
that seemed to meet, or did they,
this suspension in air that teased,
an illusion, a fragmented life transitory
like ours. Bleak in its strange beauty.
Bleak like his work on sugar plantations
and in mines that killed thousands. Bleak
like the jail from which he escaped.
Bleak his life of poverty
in Paris. I asked but no one knew his name
nor could quote a line of his poetry.
At the base of the pedestal,
carved in letters worn with age:

      Cesar Vallejo
      1892–1938

Predestination

I return to the beginning, feel
the fluid I float in, the damp

walls, red, I think, but all is dark
and I cannot be certain—perhaps

blue—perhaps black like
the undulating soul that speaks

inside my head. How do I know
all this, for I am not yet born.

My life unfolds in furrows
across my brow, in wrinkles

gathered at my fat baby
wrists. Is the tale of a life

begun before it is born?
I do not believe I cannot

determine my own path, nor
choose which buttercup I sniff, which

river I ford, which avalanche I escape.
It is best I think, to stay still,

to reabsorb into the fluid.

Collections

The people come and go
wandering among tables to and fro
choosing a rusty rim here,
a wrap-around apron there.

They gossip as they go
with neighbors and strangers,
a new acquaintance here and there,
choosing screws, nails no one else would dare.

Do they know what they do,
their arms loaded as they go?
Do I? Behind my table piled high,
choosing not to look here or there.

Among these humdrum things we go
wandering through the years to and fro.

That No-Place

I do not watch the sky darken.
I do not watch the sinking of light.
I do not watch you walking away

as though you have some place to go.
What will you do in that no-place?
There one weeds gardens,
skims clear the pond's surface,
trims the red maples
and the dark pines.

I will not watch you do these things.
They never end.

The Lion and the Lamb: A Parable

And the lion lay down with the lamb,
so they say, it being a calm day and sun
shining in golden strands like streamers

fluttering in the sky, but they do not say
how the lamb bit the lion, tore its flesh,
and blood trickled out, yes, trickled,

for the lamb is gentle and does not have
sharp teeth, but it felt the need to assert
itself over the larger creature, or at least,

to feel for a brief moment the power
of being large itself. The golden lion and
the downy white lamb lie in wait for each

other. Was this a time to spar? Or was it
a time to love? Neither the lion nor the
lamb could answer the question. For one

held power between hard cloven hooves
and the other between brisk clawed paws.
They each waited for the other to rise first.

Include at Least One Proper Name

In my family everyone loves the underground,

beneath the soil, the tribute to burial.
There is a fancy to finding Hades,

to see if it is real, to learn what scores we need
to settle before we cross over, to learn how to ask

the right questions of each other. None of us
do it. None of us know the way. How can we meet

the dark without knowing the light?

For it is dark below,
I assume.

How can we bury ourselves
before we become deft with the shovel?

Where We Go

How can you say I never speak to you?
Every time I say "I" it is you. You must
feel it. My fingertips are warm, then icy.
They are yours. As I spoke the other day,
all my "I"s caressed your name. You,
always in my thoughts, carry away my
heart in the midst of some dream, some
action in a film, some never-ending race
to the finish. I think about where we are
going and to what end. Take my hand
to let me know you are there inside my
"I," that you will go with me all the way,
even in circles.

Bradford Bog, NH

We thread through spongy peatland
protected by boards
of a different forest. We have met

after a year, my son and I, and go
immediately into our mutual
space where sky spreads over

sphagnum moss, golden thread,
sweet gale, snowberry. Little
rain has left that sky this summer

and a lone mushroom, its golden
crown glowing, edges curled
in imitation of the leaves draped

above, pops up like a small light
in this dim dense land. We continue
through Atlantic white cedars

and hemlock in step with the music
of black-capped chickadees
to the end of the boardwalk

climb weathered steps
to the observation tower
and lean on the rail.
Greens, dark and light,
reds, oranges, a sprinkling

of tiny yellow and white flowers.
As we watch
the surface expands and retracts
expands and retracts
its apparent stillness a seed within us.

We see but dimly,

he said to me, once, as he clung
between one branch of a blue-leaf tree

and another. "Sense the unfamiliar air.
Breathe all the warm you do not see,

let microbes and atoms swarm into you."
That strange air. That continuum through space.

Do all lovers live as we did?

We thought we were one but atoms
also exist in solitude, keep their distance.

If we could have seen atoms swirl
among microbes we would have been

warned against unfamiliar air. Warned
of the spaces we could fall into.

About the Author

Gayle Lauradunn writes poetry, historical fiction, short memoir, and essays. For 15 years, she worked as a freelance newspaper journalist in California and Massachusetts. She spent the summer of 1975 in residency at Cummington Community of the Arts, which included a children's program in which her five-year-old son participated. In the 1990s, she was awarded three residencies at the Virginia Center for Creative Arts. She also attended a week-long poetry workshop at the Community of Writers in Olympic Valley.

She received her BA in English Literature from the University of California, Berkeley and her PhD from University of Massachusetts, Amherst. For her PhD she created a curriculum using 20th-century U.S. poetry to teach high school students about gender, race, and class. A number of articles and workshops based on this curriculum have been published or presented. While at UMass, she taught some of the first women's courses, before there was a Women's Department on campus. She also taught politics through the arts in classes in the Honors College, the Education Department and the English Department.

Gayle was co-organizer of the first National Women's Multicultural Poetry Festival, a week-long event held at the University of Massachusetts, Amherst in March 1974. Between readings by both prestigious and little-known poets, lively discussions were held in a variety of workshops.

From 1985–1992, she served as Executive Director of the Veterans Education Project, an organization of Vietnam, Korean, and Desert Storm veterans who spoke to high school students about the realities of war and military service.

Gayle has been writing since she was nine years old. Her first poems were published in 1968 by Robert Hayden when he was poetry editor of *World Order,* a journal of the Baha'i faith, and her neighbor at Fisk University. Many of her poems have been published in print journals, online, and in national and international anthologies. Some poems were adapted and performed on stage, while others have been included in art exhibitions.

Three of her poems are in the exhibit *Dirt? Scientists, Artists, and Poets Reflect on Soil and Our Environment* held at the University of Puget Sound, then at Evergreen State College. Gayle has been invited to participate in several of the Vivo Contemporary Gallery (Santa Fe) exhibitions where the poet is paired with one of the artists and the subsequent poem is displayed beside the artwork.

From 2015–2017, she served as Chair of the Albuquerque Chapter of the New Mexico State Poetry Society. Over the years, she has given several hundred individual poetry readings in Massachusetts, Tennessee, New Hampshire, Vermont, Connecticut, New Jersey, New York City, and throughout New Mexico.

In addition to poetry, her passion is travel. She has been to all 50 states and over 40 countries; Antarctica, Bhutan, and Mongolia are her favorites.

www.ingramcontent.com/pod-product-compliance
Lightning Source LLC
Chambersburg PA
CBHW031201160426
43193CB00008B/467